C. E. WH

G000079208

Discovering
The Cinque Ports

SHIRE PUBLICATIONS LTD

ACKNOWLEDGEMENTS

Many people have helped me in the preparation of this book and to them I am very grateful. I would particularly like to thank Mrs E. Bruce-Johnston for her help and guidance.

Photographs are acknowledged as follows: Cadbury Lamb, plates 1-9, 11-13, 15, 18, 20-3, 25-6; Jane Miller, plate 10; Alan Roberton, plates 14, 16-17, 19, 24. The maps were drawn by Richard G. Holmes. The cover photograph of Mermaid Street, Rye, is by Cadbury Lamb.

Printed in Great Britain by C. I. Thomas & Sons (Haverfordwest) Ltd, Press Buildings, Merlins Bridge, Haverfordwest.

Contents

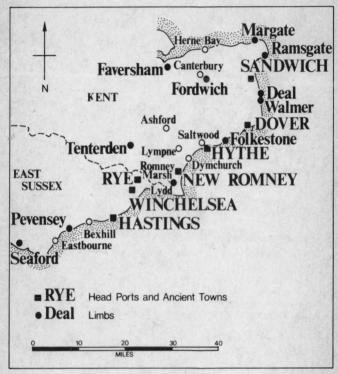

The Cinque Ports

1. Introduction

Most people have heard of the Cinque Ports but far fewer could say what the term means or what places they are. *Cinque*, pronounced *sink*, comes from the French for 'five'. The five south-east coastal towns of Hastings, New Romney, Hythe, Dover and Sandwich provided what has been claimed to be England's first organised navy.

There was probably an informal arrangement before the Norman conquest whereby the monarch granted Dover, Sandwich and Romney, at least, special rights and privileges in return for the service of boats and crews for several days each year at the ports' expense. Certainly William the Conqueror continued the arrangement, while Henry II granted charters to these ports and Hastings and Hythe individually in 1155 and 1156. They gained many privileges from these charters, including freedom to trade where they wished, the right of their own courts, 'honours at Court', the right of selected portsmen, termed 'coronation barons', to carry the canopy over the king and queen at every coronation, and a profitable but controversial right of 'den and stroud', which allowed the portsmen to land on the shore of Great Yarmouth, Norfolk, and dry their nets and sell their catch there. Big herring fairs were held at Great Yarmouth and so the Cinque Ports appointed bailiffs to superintend them. Naturally the people of Great Yarmouth resented this and there were violent incidents, even sea battles. In return for these privileges, the charters stipulated that the towns had to provide up to fifty-seven fully manned ships for the monarch's use for up to fifteen days a year. If the monarch required them for longer than fifteen days then he had to pay for the ships' upkeep.

The Cinque Ports grew in size and importance as their aid was needed to defend the coast. Their inhabitants tended to be highly independent, only willing to do what the monarch requested if they thought that it was in their own interests. Their exploits were occasionally piratical and belligerent. Edward I endeavoured to give the arrangements a formal legal footing in 1278 by issuing a Royal Charter to the Cinque Ports; it merely heightened the Ports' influence. This was further strengthened at the end of the thirteenth century when Rye and Winchelsea, the two 'Antient Towns' just inside the Sussex border, were raised to the status of Head Ports and joined the other five: the power and prestige of the Cinque Ports were at their height.

Several Kent and Sussex towns wanted to join the Cinque Ports, largely for their own protection but also for a share of the privileges. These towns were attached to various Head Ports and were called 'Limbs' or 'members'. Towns such as Folkestone were more important than other Limbs and they became 'corporate members' while lesser limbs were 'non-corporate'. A town's status might alter as it prospered or declined, though this was not common. Charles II's charter of 1668 shows seven Head Ports, seven corporate members and twenty-four non-corporate members. The members have remained more or less the same up to the present day.

Drawn together by mutual interests and enmities, the ports developed common institutions: by the middle of the twelfth century they had a joint court known as the Court of Shepway, performing for the ports as the shire court did for the county. Traditionally the meeting place was just outside Lympne, where a large stone cross, erected in 1923, marks the spot. The Court was presided over from the thirteenth century by a royal officer known as the Lord Warden of the Cinque Ports and Edward I combined the post with that of Constable of Dover Castle, as is still the case. There were two other meetings, a 'Brotherhood', which kept a watch over Cinque Ports privileges, and the 'Guestling', a meeting for Hastings, Rye and Winchelsea, probably at Guestling near Hastings. The Kent ports copied the practice, then later joint Guestlings were held. The two groups eventually combined and still meet occasionally as a 'Brotherhood and Guestling'. These days the Court of Shepway meets only to install a new Lord Warden, the last being the late Sir Robert Menzies, the former Prime Minister of Australia. As well as being Lord Warden of the Cinque Ports and Constable of Dover Castle, the incumbent of the office, which is held for life, is Admiral of the Cinque Ports, once a powerful position, but now a prestige appointment. It has had some very famous holders, such as William Pitt, the Duke of Wellington and Sir Winston Churchill. The Lord Warden's official residence is at Walmer Castle.

As early as the fourteenth century the influence of the ports was diminishing, partly because of encroaching silt or, at Hastings, erosion, and partly because naval warfare was becoming better organised. Devastating French raids left their mark, too. In spite of great efforts to keep the harbours open, only Dover continued to be a major port and by the sixteenth century the others had ceased to have any special importance.

Today the Cinque Ports have virtually no power as a group although they do retain some influence. They are a collection of historic towns and villages which are still linked by common traditions and, occasionally, colourful ceremonial: the mayors of Head Ports are the Barons when there is a coronation and they look after the flags of Commonwealth nations.

This book has been arranged so that you may visit a group of places which are particularly close together and which often have special ties. The book begins with the southernmost ports and gradually progresses up the Sussex and Kent coastline.

2. The Hastings group

SEAFORD
Population 17,720. Early closing Monday.

Although there were settlements here in the late stone age, about 1500 BC, Seaford does not seem to have been of much consequence until just after the Norman conquest, when it belonged to William de Warrenne and was becoming important as a port. It became a corporate Limb of Hastings in 1229 and as such has always been the most southerly and westerly town of the Cinque Ports organisation. By 1347 it was contributing five ships and about eighty sailors each year for the king's service. Throughout the fourteenth century in particular, Seaford, like other ports along this part of the coast, was repeatedly attacked by the French. The port declined in the sixteenth century when the river Ouse, which had hitherto flowed out into the sea beneath the cliffs at Seaford Head, changed its course, thus depriving the town of its main livelihood. Until the 1832 Reform Act the town was entitled to send two members to Parliament. William Pitt, later Prime Minister and Earl of Chatham, represented Seaford from 1747 to 1754. Another MP for Seaford was George Canning, who was Foreign Secretary and briefly Prime Minister in 1827.

The **church of St Leonard** used to be near the quayside, the river flowing where Steyne Road now is. There have been priests at the church since at least 1160. On the south side there is an interesting Norman archway, which was originally inside the church. Owing to the destruction of part of St Leonard's, possibly by marauding Frenchmen, in the fourteenth century it now forms part of the exterior.

The **Old House,** in the High Street, now an antique shop, was the home of Thomas Tufton, bailiff of Seaford, in the early eighteenth century. An inscription on the wall is dated 1712. There are interesting alleys and streets leading off the High Street, particularly Saxon Lane at the north end.

Where Chatham Place (named after Pitt) joins Steyne Road stands West House, the present **Seaford Museum,** parts of which are several hundred years old. It is open daily from Easter to September, and on Sundays and bank holidays only in the winter. Admission is free.

The **martello tower** here is the most southern and western of the towers built at the beginning of the nineteenth century as a series of watchtowers and defence points along parts of the coastline particularly threatened by the expected French invasion. Each tower had a complement of one officer and twenty-four men. The most northerly martello tower is at Folkestone.

Seaford Head can best be reached by driving down to the lower part of Seaford and joining College Road, which goes a third of the way up. Climb up to the Head itself, where the hillfort built in the iron age can still be seen as a series of mounds to the east. There are superb views both out to sea and inland.

To reach Pevensey, drive out of Seaford towards Eastbourne and turn left down the B2108 to Alfriston. The road gradually rises and 1½ miles (2.4 kilometres) along there is a stopping point on the top of the South Downs. There are dramatic views of Seaford and the sea to the south and a panoramic view to the north. Go on through Alfriston to the A27 and turn right for Pevensey.

PEVENSEY

It was probably at Pevensey rather than at Hastings that William the Conqueror landed in 1066. Pevensey was a very small village then, having grown up in the shadow of the castle which was originally built *c*. AD 340 by the Romans and was possibly the fortress of *Anderida*. Much of the Roman work can still be seen, as can the Norman additions. Pevensey was given to William the Conqueror's half-brother Robert, Count of Morain, who set about developing a port and borough outside the castle walls and repairing the structure within. By 1150, however, the port was declining as the creek gradually silted up, but for a long time it continued, as a Limb of Hastings, to send one ship for the king's service. Its date of attachment to Hastings is uncertain but was probably early in the thirteenth century.

Despite its diminutive size, Pevensey retained its mayor and corporation until the passing of the Municipal Corporation Act of 1883.

The **church** is dedicated to St Nicholas, patron saint of children and sailors, and is a complete example of the Early English style of building of the thirteenth century, though there have been extensive restorations, especially in the late nineteenth century. The muniment chest, near the Norman font, is dated 1664. There is a monument (1616) in the north aisle to John Wheatley, who was a wealthy parishioner at the time of Elizabeth I and gave a great deal of money towards the defence of England against the Spanish Armada. In the south aisle there is a glass case containing a mortar for pounding grain and two thirteenth-century coffin lids. Note, too, the bell tower at the east end of the north aisle; it has a ring of six bells, three of which are seventeenth-century.

The **castle** site was probably uninhabited when the Romans first built their fortress here *c*. AD 340. All the visible outer walls are Roman, although the Normans and others had to repair them. The castle withstood several sieges but was never stormed, although on occasions the occupants were starved out. It was last used in the Second World War, when gun emplacements and troops were installed, as an observation and command post. The keep is early twelfth-century and the inner wall and towers surrounding the keep date from the mid-thirteenth century. The castle is open from May to September daily, 9.30 to 7, and in winter on weekdays from 9.30 to 4, on Sundays from 2 to 4. It is closed over the Christmas holiday. There is an admission charge.

The tiny **Court House** in the main street was also the borough's town hall and as such claims to be the smallest in England. It is of uncertain age, though it was in existence by the seventeenth century. At one stage the borough's chief magistrate had the power to impose the death penalty. The Court House — set out inside as if for a trial — is also Pevensey's museum and has an impressive collection of items from the town's past, including the mace. The prison is directly underneath the Court House and consists of two small cells and an exercise yard. There is also an oak beam — possibly an old cell doorpost — on which some of the prisoners have left their marks. It is open from May to September daily as conditions permit, but closed in winter. The **Old Minthouse,** now an antique shop, was built in 1342, though coins were struck on this site in 1076. Edward VI is said to have stayed here. As well as the collection of minting material there is a priests' and smugglers' hiding hole. It is open from Easter to mid July, Monday to Friday, 2 to 5; mid July to mid September, weekdays and bank holidays 11 to 5, Sundays 2 to 5. A charge is made for admission.

HASTINGS
Population 74,030. Early closing Wednesday. Information centre: 4 Robertson Terrace.

Hastings's claim to be the premier Cinque Port was of long standing when the point was officially conceded in 1615, long after the town's heyday, which was towards the end of the eleventh and early in the twelfth century. Most of its history is that of the old town which is at the east end of present-day Hastings. It began as a small Saxon fishing hamlet but by AD 928 it was sufficiently important to have its own mint. It prospered under the Normans, being an important strategic town for William the Conqueror, who built a castle on the cliff above. It was also the port through which William brought Caen stone from France for Battle Abbey, which commemorates the spot where the battle of Hastings was fought, about 7 miles (11 kilometres) inland.

By the end of the twelfth century the port was beginning to be restricted by changes in the ever shifting coastline. The great storm of 1287, which destroyed old Winchelsea and wrecked Romney, virtually finished Hastings as a port, although it struggled on, a shadow of its former self, for another three hundred years. There were constant attempts to revive its possibilities until 1890, but the sea always won. The French raided the town in 1339 and 1377 and left it in such a state that Seaford, its Limb, had to provide many of the twenty-one ships required for the king's service. Part of Hastings Castle disappeared over the edge of the cliff into the encroaching sea. The French raided again in 1690.

During the nineteenth century Hastings developed as a seaside resort, although coastal erosion was still a problem: Princess Victoria, on a visit to Hastings before she became Queen, found that the sea had washed away the road in front of her carriage, which had to be dragged to the town by enthusiastic inhabitants. St Leonards, a nineteenth-century town a mile or so south-west down the coast, expanded towards Hastings and today the two are linked by a lengthy promenade, where there are amusements, a miniature railway and the White Rock Pavilion.

To reach Hastings Castle use the West Hill lift, which is in George Street, just to the west of the old town. The lift, over 460 feet (140 metres) long, operates from Easter to September. If it is not running when you go, then use the steps from Swan Terrace near St Clement's church.

At the top of the lift the path to the left leads to the **castle.** Not much is left of this Norman fortification, which has been in ruins since the sixteenth century. The huge ditch used to be a moat, 100 feet (30 metres) wide and 60 feet (18 metres) deep. The dungeons, rediscovered in 1894, should also be seen. Built against the north wall are the ruins of the Collegiate Church of the Blessed Virgin Mary, later known as the Royal Free Chapel. Thomas Becket was a former dean of the church and William of Wykeham, founder of New College, Oxford, and Winchester College, was a canon.

Across Castle Hill from the ruins is the old lighthouse. The route down to the old town starts next to it and the path to **St Clement's Caves** leads past it. The caves may be partly natural and partly man-made. They cover 3 acres (1.2 hectares) and they were used as air-raid shelters in the Second World War. They are open daily in summer, 10 to 5; winter 10 to 12.30 and 2 to 5. There is an admission charge.

Steps lead down from the lighthouse on Castle Hill to Swan Terrace and from there to the **parish church of St Clement** in the old town. The first church on this site was virtually destroyed by a French raiding party in 1377, but by the end of the century the present church had been built, an early example of the Perpendicular style. It is the oldest church in the town. On the south side of the tower, on the belfry wall, there are two seventeenth-century cannonballs embedded in the stone. One of them was fired from a French or Dutch ship or during the Civil War: the second cannonball was put up by the townsfolk in order to balance the effect! There are two chandeliers in the nave, the one nearest the chancel being made from the silver staves used by the Barons of the Cinque Ports at the coronation of George III in 1761. There are remains of the old roodscreen, a fine octagonal font carved with emblems of the Passion, and a framed reproduction of the Bayeux Tapestry.

From the church walk downhill to the High Street, which was one of the two main streets of old Hastings. Turn left and almost immediately on the left-hand side is the interesting old **Town Hall Museum.** Built in 1882, it became a museum of the town's history in 1949. It is open from Easter to September daily and in winter on Sundays only from 3 to 5. (Another museum, in John's Place in the modern part of Hastings, deals with the history and natural history of East Sussex and houses a Durbar Hall assembled by Lord Brassey.)

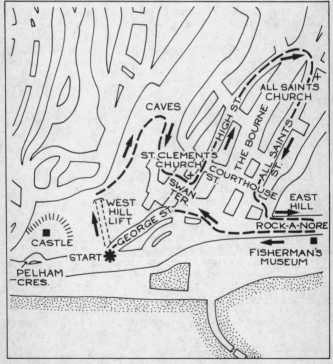

Hastings

Alleys and interesting streets lead off the High Street: Church Passage to the left, Courthouse Street to the right. A nearly hidden alleyway to the left leads almost immediately into the minute, picturesque Sinnock Square. Continue along the raised pavement until the road bends to the right and reaches an open space, opposite which is **All Saints church.** It stands at the northern end of All Saints Street, the second ancient thoroughfare of the town. In between runs the modern road called The Bourne, named after a stream which flowed through the centre of the town. The modern road cuts the old town neatly in two.

All Saints was built in 1436. A plaque notes that in 1643 it was occupied by Colonel Mosley and his Parliamentarians when they were demanding the surrender of the town. Inside the church, see the Doom painting above the chancel arch — the only survivor of a series of paintings covering the walls. The damned, most unusually, are being hanged rather than burned. A monumental brass in the south aisle commemorates one of the bailiffs of Hastings, Thomas Goodenough, and his wife Margaret, and dates from 1520. Notice the tablet on the north wall near the foot of the tower which sets out some unusual belfry rules. In the south-west corner of the tower is the old parish pump which, until 1850, was in use where Bourne Walk joins Waterloo Passage.

Continue along All Saints Street. The house on the right known as **Shovell's** is said to be the oldest house in Hastings. The mother of Admiral Sir Cloudsley Shovell lived there at the end of the seventeenth century. Further along on the left is an alley called Starr's Cottages; the first house is the curious **Piece of Cheese** — a house built to a triangular design.

At the end of All Saints Street bear left on to the Rock-a-Nore, towards the fishermen's quarter.

Some of the tall timber-built **net-shops** date from the seventeenth century and may possibly be Elizabethan. They are said to be unique to Hastings. Further on down Rock-a-Nore, the high grey building on the right is the **Fisherman's Museum** (open 1st April to 30th September every day except Fridays). It used to be the fishermen's church and contains amongst its exhibits the *Enterprise*, the last of the old Hastings luggers built for sail.

Opposite the Fisherman's Museum is **East Hill** ascended by the 272 stairs near the Dolphin Inn or by the East Hill lift (open daily May to September). At the top, the defensive ditch and earthen ramparts of a Saxon settlement can be faintly seen. Returning to Rock-a-Nore and passing back through the fishermen's quarter, cross East Parade not quite into the High Street but just to its left — into George Street where the tour started. This leads from old Hastings into the more recent parts of the town and the transition in building styles can be seen as one walks along. Further down George Street is Wellington Square and the impressive Pelham

Crescent; the first was laid out around 1815 as the first planned development of Hastings; the latter was built in 1825 by Joseph Kaye, who set his houses right into the face of Castle Hill.

3. The Winchelsea and Rye group

WINCHELSEA

Winchelsea is on the top of Iham Hill. It is a rare example of an almost complete attempt at medieval town planning, for this is the second Winchelsea: the first lies somewhere out to sea, now about two miles (three kilometres) away across the mud flats. The original town, Saxon in origin, was given, with Rye, to the abbey of Fecamp by King Canute. Henry III negotiated their return in 1246. By the end of the twelfth century both Rye and Winchelsea were Limbs of Hastings. Old Winchelsea, battered and eroded, was finally abandoned in the late thirteenth century. It had been a very successful port, like Rye, ideally placed for sailing to the English possessions in France until they were lost in 1204. By the middle of the thirteenth century it had been given the status of a Head Port of the Confederation of the Cinque Ports. In order not to upset the organisation, Rye and Winchelsea were given the style of 'Antient Towns' rather than that of Head Ports. Winchelsea's wine trade with France ensured prosperity and it was foremost among the ports in providing ship service to the King, supplying thirteen ships out of a Cinque Ports fleet of fifty in 1294.

The new Winchelsea was planned as a complete port with wharves on the river Brede. Edward I helped finance the operation, often coming down to see what was happening. This was remarkable, as Winchelsea had supported Simon de Montfort, who had earlier opposed Edward. In 1292 the townspeople thankfully moved into their new town. The streets were designed in a grid pattern of thiry-nine units but not all of them were developed. Some units were nearly 3 acres (1.2 hectares) in area and rectangular in shape. Important people were put on the north side of town and if they were merchants they were also given wharves on the Brede. New Winchelsea probably numbered six thousand people, a considerable opulation in those days. Its wine trade was important, so many of the houses were built with cellars, some of which remain.

The Hundred Years War with France (1337-1453) saw vicious raids by the French — hence the partly ruined parish church of St Thomas and the total destruction of St Giles's and other buildings in 1359. Winchelsea men and other Portsmen made equally bloody reprisal raids; no quarter was asked for or given.

By Elizabethan times the river had begun to silt up and the sea was retreating rather than advancing. Winchelsea was shrinking in size and losing prestige; it had virtually ceased to be a port. Later, it was used to accommodate French prisoners of war, who were made to cultivate flax: Winchelsea flax was famous for its fineness for a short while. The town has since shrunk still further.

Although the town is now governed by a parish council, there is also a Corporation consisting of Mayor, Jurats, Freemen, Common Clerk and Chamberlain, who look after the historic sites and buildings in Winchelsea. The Mayoring ceremony is on Easter Monday in the courthouse in the High Street.

Approaching Winchelsea from Hastings, drive into the town and park at the eastern end of the High Street. A little further on is the impressive **Strand Gate,** one of the original gates of the town, built in the late thirteenth century. There were high walls on either side. The road descends from the gate towards what was the port. A few feet on the town side of the gate note the lookout position which was used during the Napoleonic Wars. The earlier lookout, at St Thomas's church, was destroyed by marauding Frenchmen.

Starting at the Strand Gate end of the High Street, it is worth making a detour up a lane to the right, along a public footpath, and down stone steps to the **Strand Well.** Further down the High Street there is a long wall which partly hides what was Barrack Square, a name gained from army associations during the Napoleonic Wars. On the same side, on the right of Castle Road, is the only town well within the walls. It still has some of its nineteenth-century notices.

A little further down the High Street on the left are the parish church and a useful large map of the town. On the right, almost opposite the church, is the **Court Hall.** Possibly twelfth-century, this building was considerably restored in the sixteenth century. The ground floor used to be the town gaol. The upper floor, formerly the court room, is now the Winchelsea Museum, which houses a fascinating collection of local relics, photographs and mementoes. Its opening times are a little erratic although it is open most days in the summer. A small charge is made.

The **parish church of St Thomas** was given its 2½-acre (1 hectare) site by Edward I when the plans for the new town were being drawn up. It is in the early Decorated style which was becoming fashionable at the end of the thirteenth century and was magnificent, having an impressive nave with a baptistry at the west end. The tower was in the middle and some of its supporting pillars can still be seen. Much of the west end lies ruined, probably destroyed by the French in one of their raids in the fourteenth century. The chancel which remains is the finest example of the Decorated style in the country. The present west doorway is six-teenth-century.

Among the other medieval monuments note the Alard chantry on the south side. Stephen Alard was an early Admiral of the Cinque Ports Fleet, while Gervase Alard was Admiral of the Western Fleet. The original east window probably perished in a French raid. The present one is in the Perpendicular style of the

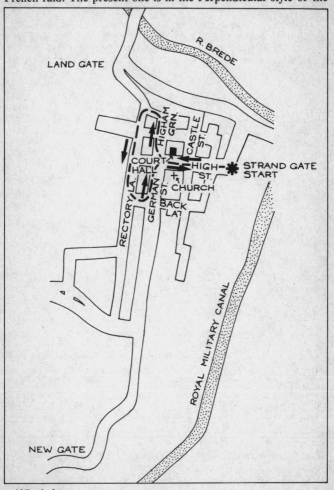

Winchelsea

15

fifteenth century. The high altar is in the same position as when the church was first built. The Farncombe chantry on the north side contains effigies that may well have been brought from Old Winchelsea church. The organ and the lovely stained glass windows by Douglas Strachan were given by Lord Blanesborough in 1931 in memory of brothers and nephews.

Outside the church, just beyond the boundary wall at the west end of the churchyard, is **Wesley's Tree.** A plaque records that it was under a similar tree on the same spot that the famous preacher gave his last open-air sermon, a few months before he died in 1791.

Leaving Wesley's Tree, turn right, passing the Court Hall, into Higham Green and at the end turn left. About 200 yards (180 metres) away is the **Pipewell** or **Land Gate**, built at the beginning of the fifteenth century over the road down to the ferry across the Brede. Until the eighteenth century the only way to Rye from Winchelsea was through this gate.

Walk on down Rectory Lane, the main road close to the Pipewell Gate, to the excavations at **Blackfriars** ruins. The Black Friars came to Winchelsea in 1318 but lost their property at the dissolution of the monasteries in Henry VIII's reign.

On the opposite side of the road is a small Wesleyan chapel built in 1786. Wesley himself preached there. Turn left down Back Lane to return to the church, stopping at **Manna Platt** in Mill Road to look at the fine fourteenth-century vaulted cellar.

There is a beautiful, though lengthy, tree-lined walk down German Street along what is called Monk's Walk. On the left is Grey Friars, once the property of the order, now rebuilt and an old people's home. Continue out of the town to the junction with the Hastings road and turn left. Over to the right, a ruined gable is all that remains of **St John's Hospital,** built for the new Winchelsea in 1292 for both men and women and dissolved in Henry VIII's reign. Half a mile down the country lane to Pett is **New Gate,** where the boundary of the town was to be.

Off the Royal Military Road between Winchelsea and Rye, down the road to Winchelsea Beach is **Camber Castle,** also known as Winchelsea Castle. It was built in the 1530s and 1540s by Henry VIII, quickly fell into decay and was ordered to be dismantled by Charles I in 1626. The order was never carried out. It was under repair at the time of writing and not open to the public.

RYE

Population 4450. Early closing Tuesday. Market day Thursday. Tourist information : Perry Road.

Rye, one of the most enchanting of the Cinque Port towns, is one of the two 'Antient Towns' added to the original five Head Ports of the Confederation about 1336. Rye was part of the gift by

King Canute to the French abbey of Fecamp, later redeemed by Henry III. Like Winchelsea, Rye was a gateway to France for several centuries, especially to the English lands held there. During the Hundred Years War with France in the fourteenth century Rye was attacked with considerable ferocity: it was sacked in 1339, raided again in 1377 when the church bells were taken, and once more in 1385. Rye retaliated vigorously and successfully retrieved the church bells.

In the sixteenth century and again in 1685, hundreds of persecuted French Huguenots emigrated to Rye. They bolstered a population that was declining as the river had begun to silt up badly, making it impossible for more modern, larger ships to use the port, though the fishing and boatbuilding industries continued. Rye is now a picturesque resort and market town whose trade is augmented by craft industries, notably pottery.

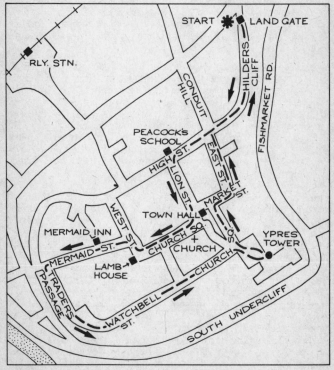

Rye

Entering Rye from the Winchelsea end, follow the road round, past the windmill on the left, and then along South Undercliff and Fishmarket Road. Car parks are at the junction of Fishmarket Road and New Road. A footpath leads to the **Landgate.** Built in 1329, complete with drawbridge and portcullis, the Landgate (the gate on the landward side) is the only main gate still standing in Rye and marks the line of the old town wall. Follow Hilders Cliff Road round and up to the High Street, the hub of commercial life in Rye. To the right, just past the Custom House, is Conduit Hill, which used to have a small postern gate at the bottom; down here may be found an old Augustinian friary, now a pottery. Further down the High Street, on the same side, is the Old Grammar School, or **Peacock's School,** mentioned by Thackeray in *Denis Duval*. A fine brick building with Dutch gables, it was built in 1636 and used as a school until 1908. A modern comprehensive school called Peacock's is on the north side of the town. On the other side of the street, almost opposite the school, is the George Inn, which still possesses a minstrels' gallery. It adjoins Lion Street, at the top of which are the Town Hall and St Mary's church.

The **Town Hall** was built in 1742, the ground floor arcade providing space for a small market. The first floor was a magistrates' court as well as a council chamber; the handsome room contains interesting town relics — the mayor's bell of 1565, a pair of maces, and gibbet chains with a real skull. On Mayoring Day hot pennies used to be flung down to the children.

Between the Town Hall and the church is **Fletcher's House,** originally the vicarage, where the dramatist John Fletcher (1579-1625) was born, son of Richard Fletcher, who later became Bishop of London.

From the north side, the first notable feature of **St Mary's church** is the clock, complete with quarter boys. Made in 1560, it is reputed to be the oldest turret clock in Britain still functioning with its original works. The remarkable 18 foot (5.49 metres) pendulum swings inside the church. The quarter boys, originally installed in 1760, were replaced by copies in 1971. The originals are in the north chapel.

This memorable church, sometimes called the cathedral of East Sussex, has a chancel which dates from *c.* 1120. Most of the church was built *c.* 1180 although the north or Clere Chapel is thirteenth-century. The unusual flying buttresses at the east end reach down to the ground. Like Winchelsea, this church suffered from French raids, particularly that of 1377. The communion table (*c.*1730) in the north chapel is beautifully carved. The west-end window was presented in 1937 by E. F. Benson, the novelist and a former mayor, in memory of his parents, Archbishop and Mrs Benson. He can be seen in mayoral robes in the bottom right-hand corner. There is a Burne-Jones window in the north aisle. To the north of the font in the north nave aisle are examples of early bibles and prayer-books. The screen which separates the transepts from the chapels is probably part of the original roodscreen dating from the fifteenth century. The organ was installed in 1901. There is access to the clock and bells on weekdays: details on enquiry.

On the north-west corner of Church Square there is an old house with a crooked chimney. This is Grene Hall, where Elizabeth I is supposed to have stayed during her visit to Rye in 1573. Nearby, in West Street, is **Lamb House** (National Trust; open April to the end of October, Wednesdays and Saturdays, 2 to 6). The Lamb family produced numerous mayors of Rye. From 1898 to 1918 the writer Henry James lived there. Follow the road round to **Mermaid Street** on the left, steep and cobbled, one of the most attractive streets in southern England. The **Mermaid Inn,** dating from the fifteenth century, has fine wall paintings and a vaulted cellar. Further down the street on the same side is Hartshorn House, which became a hospital during the Napoleonic Wars.

Just before the end of Mermaid Street turn left into picturesque Traders Passage and walk through to **Watchbell Street,** so called because of the alarm or Watchbell that was kept in this street to warn of French raids. The most interesting house, the **Old Stone House**, is at the top of the street, where Church Square is rejoined. It was one of the few dwellings spared in the French raid of 1377 and was originally part of the buildings of the Friars of the Sack, who built it in 1263. The order was dissolved in 1307. The building was modernised in 1869. Almost opposite is St Anthony's House, a carefully restored example of fifteenth-century work.

Walk back through Church Square, keeping St Mary's on the left, to the formidable **Ypres Tower** overlooking the harbour. Originally known as Baddyngs Tower, it was said to have been built by Peter of Savoy during the reign of Henry III in the thirteenth century in the south-east angle of the town fortifications. In 1430 the corporation sold it to John Yprys and in 1518 they bought it back, using it as a gaol until 1891. It now houses Rye Museum (open Easter to mid October, weekdays 10.30 to 1, 2.15 to 5.30; Sundays 11.30 to 1, 2.15 to 5.30). There is an admission charge. The Gun Garden below mounted a gun battery until Elizabethan times.

Walk back on the east side of Church Square and Rye's **Water House** can be seen. It was built in 1735 in order to bring water up to the town. Eventually Market Street is reached, with the **Flushing Inn** to the right. The vaulted cellar was traditionally a store for contraband spirits.

Follow Market Street round to East Street at the end of which is the High Street and turn right to reach the Landgate.

From Rye, journeying northward on the A259 to Tenterden, bear left and join the B2082. Follow this road and where it turns sharp left just before Wittersham a windmill will be seen which is sometimes open to the public. Continue to **Small Hythe,** which used to be the port for Tenterden. The old harbour house, dating from the late fifteenth century, will be seen on the right. Here Dame Ellen Terry, the distinguished actress, lived for twenty-five years. It is now a National Trust museum devoted to Dame Ellen and the theatre of her day. It is open March to October except Tuesdays and Fridays, 2 to 6 or dusk. There is an admission charge. Tenterden is two miles further down the same road.

TENTERDEN
Population 5930. Early closing Wednesday. Market day Friday.

Tenterden, Kent, is remarkable in that it is the only incorporated member of the Cinque Ports whose Head Port, Rye, is in a different county — Sussex. Tenterden was far up one of the small creeks that existed along the coast in the eleventh and twelfth centuries. Small Hythe was its port, on the river Rother. Small Hythe was famed for its shipbuilding even as late as the mid sixteenth century but within a short time the river silted up too badly to allow further trade by water. Tenterden had an excellent reputation in the wool trade established by Flemings in the fourteenth century. The town was run by a bailiff but was granted a mayor in 1600. It became an incorporated Limb of Rye in 1449 and, after 1600, an important market town. The main street is particularly attractive, being broad and tree-lined, with many eighteenth-century buildings.

The **church,** just off the High Street, is dedicated to St Mildred. It was complete by the sixteenth century but some of its arcading is thirteenth-century. The fine west tower, formerly used as a beacon tower, has a famous ring of bells, while the nave has a wagon ceiling and is remarkable for being roofed with shingles. In the north aisle there is a fourteenth-century alabaster panel of the Resurrection.

The **Kent and East Sussex Light Railway** was the first standard-gauge line to be built under the Act of 1896 and was opened between 1900 and 1905. It was closed to passengers in 1954 and to all traffic in 1961. Enthusiasts bought a ten-mile stretch of line (16 kilometres) with the necessary rolling stock and reopened part of it to passengers in 1974. Eventually it is hoped to provide a service through the Rother valley, terminating at Bodiam Castle.

The **Local History Collection** is housed between the railway station and the High Street. It is not yet a full-blown museum but nonetheless there are some interesting exhibits.

Leaving Tenterden for New Romney, take the B2080, from which there are some superb views of Romney Marsh to the left.

4. Romney Marsh and New Romney

ROMNEY MARSH

Romney Marsh, an area of roughly 50,000 acres (20,000 hectares), lies between Rye and Hythe, bounded by the sea to the south and east and by the Royal Military Canal to the north. It is renowned for its flatness and excellent soil, like the Fens of East Anglia, and has its own breed of sheep and type of frogs! The Marsh developed gradually as a result of the silting up of rivers such as the Rother, together with the deposition of shingle along the coastline, notably at Dungeness.

The powerful Lords of the Marsh, who administered the area, were often in conflict with their counterparts of the Cinque Ports and in constant battle with the sea. New Romney was in a difficult diplomatic position, being both on the Marsh and a Head Port of the Cinque Ports.

There are small villages with majestic churches, usually far too big for their present congregations. With its dykes and sluices, streams and rivulets, it was ideal country for the 'owlers' or smugglers, particularly in the eighteenth and nineteenth centuries. Along the coast from Hastings to Sandwich such activities were rife but the Marsh was perhaps the busiest of all. Today the ten villages which make up the heart of Romney Marsh are grouped under one huge parish — a tour for church enthusiasts.

Fairfield

Off the A259, the small church dedicated to St Thomas of Canterbury stands by itself. Beautifully restored in 1912-13, parts of it may be eleventh-century. It has a three-decker pulpit and black and white box pews.

Brookland

The village and the church are on the A259 from Rye to New Romney. St Augustine's, built in the thirteenth century, though with later additions, is well known because of its curious detached wooden bell-tower of tiered construction. The church is attractive, with box pews and a twelfth-century lead font showing signs of the Zodiac.

Brenzett

The church of St Eanswith dates from the thirteenth and fourteenth centuries; restoration in 1892 was unsympathetic. The church contains a monument to two Roundheads and an eighteenth-century reredos.

Snargate

On the B2080 between Brenzett and Appledore, the church probably dates from the late thirteenth century, though the tower is later. It was used as a smugglers' store, probably with the connivance of the incumbent. Richard H. Barham, author of *Ingoldsby Legends,* began his writing while rector here.

Snave

On the B2081 from Brenzett, the church of St Augustine dates back to Norman times, although it was largely rebuilt in the fifteenth and early sixteenth centuries.

Newchurch

Two miles north-east of the B2070 at Ivychurch is the large church of St Peter and St Paul, with a thirteenth-century chancel and a fifteenth-century tower which leans a little. Note the intertwined roses of Lancaster and York on the font shields. The late thirteenth-century vestment chest is now the altar in the north chapel.

Burmarsh

Two miles north-west of Dymchurch, All Saints is basically Norman with an interesting south doorway and a fine fifteenth-century west tower.

St Mary-in-the-Marsh

Between Dymchurch and Ivychurch, the church is of Norman origin but was clearly much rebuilt in the thirteenth century. It is double-aisled and has two interesting brasses from 1449 and 1502. E. Nesbitt, the well-known writer, is buried in the churchyard.

Ivychurch

The superb church was built *c.* 1370 and the 100-foot (30 metre) tower a little later. It was requisitioned as sleeping quarters and stables in the Civil War. What appears to be a watchman's box is a 'hudd' used by the priest at the graveside on rainy days.

Old Romney

On the A259, Old Romney was a busy port on the Rother before it silted up in the thirteenth century. In 1377 there were only 133 people left. Romney, now called New Romney, the Head Port, had a population of 1500 by then. St Clement's is the only church still standing in the village and dates from the thirteenth century. Its font, which is in the Decorated style, has most unusual carving on its supports.

NEW ROMNEY

Population 3540. Early closing Wednesday.

New Romney may be thought of as being on the Marsh but not of the Marsh. Granted a mayor in 1563 — the town had had a bailiff responsible to the Archbishop of Canterbury until then — New Romney had been a Head Port of the Cinque Ports for at least two centuries and had been in opposition to the Lords of the Marsh on several occasions when Cinque Port and Marsh views conflicted.

New Romney probably existed in Saxon times when it may have been called *Romenal*. The prefix *New* does not appear until 1567, possibly when the population of Old Romney was forced to move when the river Rother silted up. They were unwise, for New Romney had already declined as a port because the Great Storm of 1287 had finally altered the course of the river Rother by several miles to the thriving port of Rye, and although New Romney tried innumerable times to coax the river back all attempts were unsuccessful. In 1347 the town sent four ships to the siege of Calais. In 1351 it was unable to find its quota and lost its privileges as a Cinque Port for a short while.

The town had an important part to play in the Cinque Ports Confederation. Centrally placed on the Kent and Sussex coastline, it became the accepted venue for the Brotherhood and a repository for official documents. Until 1971 New Romney held the records of such meetings from the fifteenth century to the present day in the White and Black Books. They are now kept by the county archivist at Maidstone. Earlier records going back to 1353 are at St Catherine's College, Cambridge.

New Romney is probably smaller than it was; it had its own mint, until 1882 sent two members to Parliament and had three churches and two religious houses. Today there is only the parish church of St Nicholas. Several streets to the north of New Romney no longer exist. However, the resort of Littlestone-on-Sea, which was laid out in 1886 and is close to the old port, could be taken as an extension of it.

The **parish church of St Nicholas** has a solid, magnificent Norman west tower, a landmark of the Marsh, though much of the church is late fourteenth-century in the Decorated style. The sedilia in the chancel and side chapels are most interesting, as is the 1602 screen. There are a number of imposing tombs, particularly the table-tomb of Richard Stuppenye in the south aisle. Around this tomb the mayor was elected from 1622 until well into the nineteenth century, when an Act of Parliament forbade the practice.

The **Romney, Hythe and Dymchurch Light Railway** runs fascinating trains, one third full-size, with ten steam locomotives and seventy-five passenger coaches, the inspiration of Captain J.

E. P. Howey. The railway was started in 1925 and the first stretch was opened in 1927. The line runs 14 miles (22.5 kilometres) from Dungeness Lighthouse to Hythe. At New Romney there are yards, workshops and a model exhibition.

The Town Hall used to have a considerable number of interesting items on display, but many of them have been moved to Maidstone.

LYDD

Lydd was originally on an island but as rivers silted up and shingle piled up around the shoreline so Lydd became part of the mainland, perhaps as early as AD 740. East Field, close to Lydd, was given by King Offa to Archbishop Jaenbert in 774. By the ninth century it had a harbour and by the mid twelfth century it was an incorporated member of the Cinque Ports. Its Head Port was New Romney, for which Lydd provided one fifth of the required ship service. Shingle finally destroyed Lydd as a port. It has been granted several charters, the first by Edward III in 1364. The town had a bailiff until incorporation in 1885, when it became entitled to a mayor. In 1888 a new explosive tested at the nearby ranges was named 'Lyddite'.

All Saints church is often called the cathedral of the Marshes. The tower, early fifteenth-century, is over 130 feet high (40 metres). The rest of the church is mainly thirteenth-century but there are remains of a Saxon church in the north aisle. It was badly damaged during the Second World War and the chancel has since been carefully rebuilt. The most distinguished rector was Thomas Wolsey, later a cardinal, who was an absentee incumbent from 1503 to 1514.

DYMCHURCH

Dymchurch was the seat of government of Romney Marsh. The Lords of the Level — the Lords, Bailiff and Jurats of Romney Marsh — would meet in New Hall to discuss how to protect the coast from flooding, as erosion was occurring from Rye to Dungeness and from Dymchurch to Hythe. In the thirteenth, sixteenth and nineteenth centuries considerable defences were built but it was not until the 1950s that substantial walls were erected. Dymchurch never belonged to the Cinque Ports. These days it is a crowded resort, celebrated as the haunt of Russell Thorndike's fictional parson-smuggler, Dr Syn.

New Hall dates from 1580 and replaced a building destroyed by fire. Now a small museum, it contains amongst other items a copy of a charter of Henry III. It also has a small prison, as New Hall was the courthouse of the Lords of Romney Marsh, who still meet

24

there once a year for their Grand Lath or meeting, although they have few powers.

The **parish church of St Peter and St Paul** has some original Norman walls and a notable chancel arch. The chancel is Early English in style.

5. The Hythe area

HYTHE

Population 12,210. Early closing Wednesday. Covered market Friday.

The name *Hythe* comes from the Saxon for 'haven' or 'resting place'. Hythe developed when the old Roman port of *Portus Lemanis*, present-day Lympne, became silted up. Hythe was part of the manor of Saltwood, a village further up the hill. The manor was probably granted to Christ Church, Canterbury, by one of Canute's thanes, and consequently it came into the possession of the Archbishop of Canterbury. He appointed a bailiff to govern Hythe. It remained with the Archbishops until surrendered to Henry VIII by Cranmer in 1541. In 1575 Elizabeth I granted Hythe a charter allowing the people their own mayor but it was not until 1844 that Hythe parish became separate from Saltwood.

Hythe was confirmed as a Cinque Port by charter from Henry II in 1155, and another from Edward I in 1278 named Hythe as a Head Port. The town was at the zenith of its importance and influence in the thirteenth century and this is reflected in the massive expansion of the church, even though it had chapel-of-ease status. Yet the town never enjoyed the prosperity of Rye, Winchelsea or Sandwich.

Hythe performed its ship-service intermittently, sending only five ships on some occasions, although eleven were supplied to defeat the Armada in 1588. The inhabitants fought off two hundred French invaders in 1293 but were not always so lucky. They suffered the Black Death in 1348, a fire in 1400 and another plague soon after, while about the same time a hundred Hythe men in five ships were lost at sea. Henry IV consequently excused the port ship-service and other obligations until the portsmen could rebuild their community.

Despite determined efforts, by 1634 Hythe had ceased to be a port because of silt. The vulnerability of Romney Marsh, should Napoleon invade, induced the government to set up martello towers, of which there are several near Hythe, and cut the Royal Military Canal from Hythe to Winchelsea, to isolate the Marsh from the mainland.

Hythe ceased to be a borough in 1973 but has retained a town mayor and corporation. A tour around the town begins with the easily distinguishable parish church on the hillside. The nave of **St Leonard's** is late Norman but the chancel was substantially altered and additions were made in the thirteenth century, creating a fine example of Early English design. The chancel is awe-inspiring. Approached by nine wide steps, it is 4 feet (1.2 metres) above the nave, with richly decorated columns. The limits of the hillside site obliged the architect to build a passage under the chancel to complete the circular processional route around the church required by medieval liturgy. The chancel vaulting was not completed until 1887.

The three-manual organ, on the south side of the choir, is by Harrison and Harrison and was completed in 1936. Although most of the pipes are at the west end, there is also a choir organ in the north triforium operated from the same console.

In the vestry, on the north side of the nave, is a superb Norman doorway with zigzag ornament and an unusual marquetry table which was probably the sounding board of an eighteenth-century pulpit. In the south nave aisle is a brass plaque to John Bridgeman, the last bailiff and first mayor of Hythe. Over the south porch is the old Town Hall, where the corporation met until their Town Hall was completed in 1794. The church still pays 5p annual rent for it.

The ambulatory, often referred to as the Crypt, is famous for its collection of human bones, which are probably medieval. It is open in summer from 2 to 4. There is an admission charge.

In the churchyard is the tomb of Lionel Lukin, inventor of the lifeboat.

From the south porch of the church, turn sharp right past the Vicarage and down Oak Walk. At the end is Church Hill. Turn left, descending the hill. This is one of the oldest and most attractive thoroughfares in Hythe. Bartholomew Street is soon reached; on the corner is an old house called **Centuries.** Enlarged in the nineteenth century, this building was first mentioned in 1276 as St Bartholomew's Hospital for old and sick townspeople. Its name has been united with St John's Hospice in the High Street which carries on this ancient charity, looking after poor, elderly and single residents of the town. Continue down the hill to the High Street.

Cross the High Street and turn right at Prospect Road. Just around the corner is a bridge crossing the **Royal Military Canal**, which runs from Seabrook, east of Hythe, to the river Rother near Rye. When Napoleon was preparing to invade England in 1805, it was thought his army might land at Romney Marsh. As well as building the martello towers a 27-mile (43.5 kilometre) canal was dug in order to isolate the Marsh, turning it into an island. It performed the same function in the Second World War. The canal has a kink at every third of a mile, to enable the batteries on the

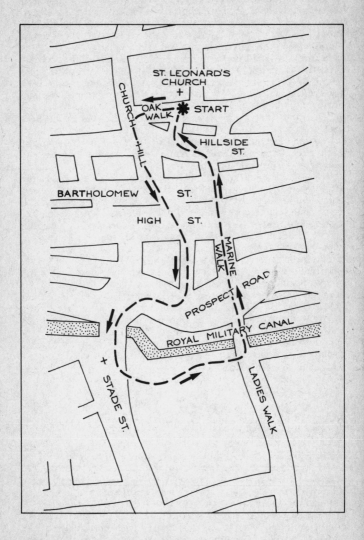

Hythe

north bank to cover each stretch of water. There was a system of sluices which could flood the whole Marsh within two tides.

Today the canal is very attractive with trees and grass banks. Every two years Hythe holds a Venetian Fete, when numerous illuminated floats pass along this part of the canal.

Passing over the canal bridge and into Stade Street, on the left, is **Oaklands.** This is the town clerk's department, local library and museum, which has a copy of Edward I's charter and also Elizabeth's charter of 1575. The museum is free and is open during normal office hours. Return to the canal via Oaklands gardens and, turning right, walk down by the canal to the next bridge.

Before crossing the bridge look right; there is a lovely avenue of wych elms known as Ladies Walk, which commemorates the Jubilee of George III in 1810.

Back over the canal, cross Prospect Road, and go up Marine Walk to the High Street: the White Hart Hotel on the north side is over three hundred years old and next to it, prudently joined by a side door, is the eighteenth-century Town Hall. The fourteenth-century **Hospital of St Bartholomew and St John** is further along on the south side of the High Street. Ascending the hill by the passage by the Town Hall and quickly passing over Bartholomew Street, Hillside Street is reached.

Turn left here and on the left is the old **Manor House,** where the Deedes family, known today in politics and journalism, lived for hundreds of years. They rebuilt the south transept of the church in 1741 and eventually moved to Sandling Park, just outside Hythe. Before returning to the church it is worth walking further down Hillside Street.

The Romney, Hythe and Dymchurch Light Railway has its eastern terminus at Hythe (see under New Romney).

Saltwood Castle

North of Hythe lies Saltwood, on top of the hill, Saltwood Castle is owned by the Hon. Alan Clark, MP, son of Lord Clark, the distinguished art historian.

The moated castle had an outer and an inner bailey. Originally a residence of the Archbishops of Canterbury including St Thomas Becket, it was confiscated by the Crown during the Archbishop's quarrel with Henry II. It was here that the four knights stayed the night before they murdered St Thomas in Canterbury Cathedral.

The castle was restored to the Archbishop of Canterbury by King John. Archbishop Courtney made it his main residence in 1382. Archbishop Cranmer surrendered it to Henry VIII, who passed it to Thomas Cromwell. During the sixteenth century it was the residence of the Lord Warden of the Cinque Ports. It descended through many families to its present-day owners. Both Edward II and Elizabeth I are said to have visited it.

LYMPNE

Three miles from Hythe is Lympne, the Roman *Portus Lemanis*, port of the Limen (Rother), built to protect the coast against Saxon invaders. **Lympne Castle** is on the clifftop next to the Norman parish church. The modern house incorporates parts of a fortified manor of the early fifteenth century which belonged to the Archdeacons of Canterbury. Lympne was made over to the Archdeacons in the eleventh century by Archbishop Lanfranc, who founded the church. The castle is open from April to October on Wednesdays and Sundays, daily from July to September, and on bank holidays, 10.30 to 6, and by appointment. There is a spectacular view over Romney Marsh. Beneath the cliff are remains of the Roman fortifications, called Stutfall Castle, which cover about ten acres. It is difficult to imagine that there was a port here.

The road to Tenterden passes **Port Lympne,** a beautiful country house whose grounds have been recently turned into a wildlife park. The house was built by Sir Philip Sassoon at the beginning of this century and it was here that allied leaders met in 1921 to discuss German reparations.

Outside Lympne, on the Hythe road, is the **Shepway Cross** erected in 1923 by the then Lord Warden and Admiral of the Cinque Ports, the Earl of Beauchamp. Here the Court of Shepway met to discuss Cinque Ports matters, fourteenth-century records specifically naming the spot. There are dramatic views over Romney Marsh.

6. Folkestone and Dover

FOLKESTONE

Population 45,610. Early closing Wednesday. Market days Tuesday and Friday. Information kiosk: Sandgate Road Pedestrian Precinct.

The origins of Folkestone are uncertain, perhaps pre-Roman. Romans lived close by but it was the Saxons who established a community. Earl Godwin attacked it in the eleventh century, virtually destroying the settlement and St Eanswythe's convent, which was named after the founder, a daughter of the King of Kent. After the Conquest, the Domesday Book valued Folkestone at £100. A priory established on the site of the old convent was resited in 1138, destroyed in 1216 and rebuilt about 1220 — the beginning of the present parish church.

A Limb of Dover, Folkestone was given a charter of Cinque Ports incorporation in 1313. The town was partly destroyed by a combined French and Scots raid in 1378 from which it took years to recover. By the late eighteenth century it had begun to be an elegant resort, although it had been a smugglers' haunt. Its importance increased with the coming of the railway and the expansion of the harbour for increased cross-channel traffic. Lord Radnor, who owned the area, began to develop the town. In the First World War it was the main embarkation point for France. It has retained its town mayor with Charter Trustees, although in 1973 it came under Shepway District Council.

The **Stade,** the fishermen's quarter of Folkestone for hundreds of years, was rebuilt early this century and the narrow streets around the harbour were badly damaged by bombs during the war. Look at the harbour, which was originally completed in 1809, much of it to Thomas Telford's instructions in collaboration with William Jessop. Move westwards and cross Harbour Street into the old **High Street**. This narrow, cobbled street, leading to the higher parts of the town, is still picturesque. At the top, on the right, is a leather shop where leatherworkers can be seen at work, and next door visitors can watch Folkestone rock being made.

Turn left at the end of the High Street, following the narrow road around to the **Bayle,** a short form of 'bailey', a Norman word for the castle which once existed here, built perhaps by the Saxon king Eadbald. This is the oldest part of the town, with some quaint cottages and the British Lion inn. Follow the Bayle round to the right to the **parish church of St Mary and St Eanswythe.**

St Eanswythe, daughter of King Eadbald of Kent, founded a nunnery on the clifftop at Folkestone in AD 630. Unfortunately the sea undermined the cliff; a new monastery was built, was undermined in its turn and the foundations of the present church were begun in 1138 to house St Eanswythe's relics. The church was sacked in 1216 by the French, rebuilt in 1220 and again in 1236. The north side was enlarged in 1474 and the nave was rebuilt in 1864. The chancel chapels are late fifteenth-century. The central tower is Perpendicular in style. The west window was subscribed by English doctors in memory of William Harvey, who was born in Folkestone in 1578 and who discovered the circulation of the blood.

From the north door turn sharp left, following the path round to Albion Villas and the Leas. A plaque at No. 3 Albion Villas shows where Charles Dickens lived in 1855. Ahead is the promenade for which Folkestone is famous — the **Leas,** built in the nineteenth century. The water lift, similar to those at Hastings, was opened in 1885. The massive Leas Cliff Hall, built into the side of the cliff, was opened in 1927 by Prince Henry. Almost opposite the hall is a statue to William Harvey. Follow the Leas to the end, go down some steps, turn left at the bottom and cross the road to **H. G. Wells's house,** which is open daily to the public. Built in 1899, Spade House was the place where *Love and Mr Lewisham, Kipps, War in the Air* and *The History of Mr Polly* were written.

Back at the Albion Villas end of the Leas, turn right into West Terrace, and right again into the pedestrian precinct. Near the middle of this precinct is an English cannonball embedded in French rock, which was brought back to England by representatives of Boulogne, long after it was fired in 1544. There is also a 150-year-old Dutch paving brick given by the town of Middelburg. Follow Sandgate Road down to the bottom, passing the 1861 Town Hall, and turn into Rendezvous Street. Follow it round to Grace Hill, where are the library and museum.

The **museum** has archaeological, natural history and local history exhibits. It is open Monday to Saturday (not bank holidays), 10 to 6 April to September, 10 to 5 the other months (Wednesday 10 to 1). Admission is free. The library is also the local archive centre. From the library return to Rendezvous Street, left into the old High Street and back to the Stade.

Walk east from the Stade towards East Cliff, to **martello towers** numbers one, two and three, the most northern and easterly of the chain built in 1805, when Napoleon threatened invasion, as

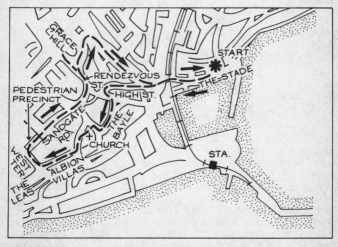

Folkestone

both fortification and lookout points. They stretch round the coast to Seaford, Sussex.

Almost overshadowing Folkestone are the chalk North Downs, from which there are superb panoramic views of the town and the surrounding countryside. One high point, known as **Caesar's Camp,** is a Norman earthwork.

Leave Folkestone by the Canterbury Road (A260) and about half a mile along the road turn right on to the B2060. The road wanders through the lovely Alkham valley. Near Dover, glimpse the beautiful Russell Gardens on the left and the equally attractive Kearsney Abbey gardens a little further on the right.

Just before entering Dover, the Alkham road turns sharp left beyond a railway bridge. Take the minor road on the right which leads to **Crabble Mill,** an early nineteenth-century watermill for grinding corn, now restored to working order. There are displays showing aspects of milling. It is open from Easter to mid September on Wednesdays and Saturdays from 2 to 5. Children up to fourteen must be accompanied. On Sundays and bank holidays (open 10 to 1, and 2 to 6) the machinery operates and children under fourteen are not admitted. An admission fee is charged.

DOVER
Population 34,322. Early closing Wednesday. Market day Saturday. Information centre: Town Hall. Tourist information : Town Wall Street.

Dover has been the 'Gateway of England' since Roman times. The fort of *Dubris* was the probable headquarters of the Roman fleet in the second and third centuries. This Cinque Head Port, the only one to remain a port, is today the busiest of the cross-channel points of embarkation.

Since Roman times, Dover has been of key strategic significance in the kingdom's defences. Fortifications attributed to Harold were enclosed by a Norman castle, though the first stonework was probably built by Henry II. William I's half-brother Odo, Bishop of Bayeux, became Lord of Dover Castle and Earl of Kent. Dover supplied the king with twenty ships. Under King John, the Constable of the Castle was Hubert de Burgh, who successfully defended it against rebellious barons and the French. De Burgh later succeeded, with Cinque Ports ships, in defeating a French invasion fleet. In Edward III's reign, a large number of Frenchmen landed and burnt Dover though the castle garrison retaliated and drove them out. Although the town was Yorkist in the Wars of the Roses, Henry VIII and Elizabeth I did much for Dover, helping to rebuild the harbour, which was in danger of silting up, and putting the town on a better financial footing.

In the Civil War, Dover Castle was held for the King but in 1642 it was taken over and kept with little trouble by Parliamentarians,

1. Pevensey. The Old Minthouse seen through the arch of the east gate of the Roman fortress.

2. Hastings. The ruined Norman castle stands on a clifftop above the town.

3. Hastings. The Fisherman's Museum is housed in a former church amongst the timber net-shops, a unique feature of the town.

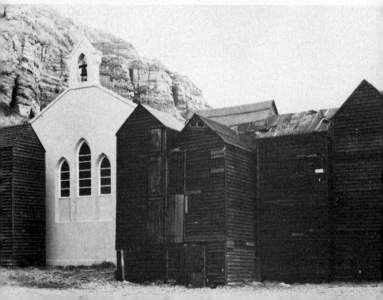

4. Hastings. Pelham Crescent is an impressive terrace of houses built in 1825 and set into the face of Castle Hill.

5. Winchelsea. The New Gate, half a mile down a country lane, marks the originally planned boundary of the town.

6. Winchelsea. The Strand Gate was one of the town's original gates, built in the thirteenth century.

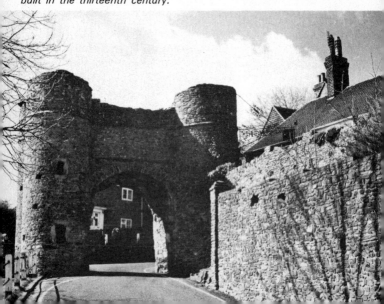

7. Winchelsea. The parish church of St Thomas is a fine example of the Decorated style, although it was partly destroyed by French raiders.

8. Rye. The windmill, of the smock type, stands on the riverbank near the railway line.

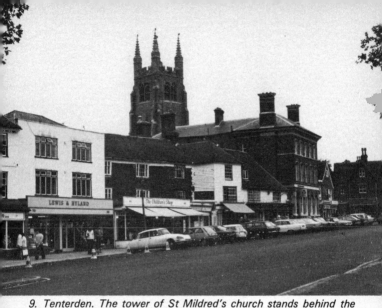

9. *Tenterden. The tower of St Mildred's church stands behind the attractive buildings of the High Street.*

10. *Romney Marsh. St Augustine's church, Brookland, has an unusual tiered wooden bell-tower.*

11. New Romney. The fine doorway of the parish church of St Nicholas.

12. The Romney, Hythe and Dymchurch Light Railway runs fourteen miles from Hythe to Dungeness. This train is seen at Dymchurch.

13. Dymchurch. A cannon at the martello tower.

14. The Shepway Cross near Lympne was erected in 1923 at the place where the Court of Shepway met to discuss Cinque Ports affairs.

15. Hythe. The Royal Military Canal, which passes through the town, was built as a protection against invasion by Napoleon.

16. Hythe. St Leonard's parish church has a Norman nave and a fine
Early English chancel.

17. *Folkestone. Handsome old houses border the churchyard.*

18. *Folkestone. In the High Street is this ancient shop where rock and humbugs are made and sold.*

19. Dover. The Pharos, or Roman lighthouse, is claimed to be the oldest standing building in Britain.

20. *Dover. The aeroplane in the turf marks the landing place in 1909 of Louis Bleriot when he became the first man to fly the English Channel.*

21. *Dover. The castle overlooks the modern shopping centre.*

22. Deal. The ball and shaft on the roof of the Time Ball Tower were used each day to communicate the correct time to ships.

23. *Sandwich. Timber-framed buildings in one of the town's many delightful streets.*

24. *Sandwich. The Tollbridge and Tudor Barbican or Bridge Gate.*

25. Walmer Castle, one of three in the area built by Henry VIII, is the official residence of the Lord Warden of the Cinque Ports.

26. Faversham. The Guildhall, built c. 1570 as a market hall but converted to its present use in 1604, was rebuilt in 1819.

even though the town was predominantly Royalist in sympathy. It was surrendered to the Earl of Winchelsea for King Charles II in 1660. The King subsequently authorised £30,000 to be spent on the harbour.

Additional defences were built on the Western Heights to counter Napoleonic threats of invasion, and then during the Second World War.

The Lord Warden of the Cinque Ports — who is also the Constable of Dover Castle — is admitted to his offices in Dover in three separate events on the same day. First of all there is an inspection of a guard of honour and the handing over of the keys of the castle at the castle. This is followed by the formal installation of the Lord Warden into that office by the Court of Shepway; this takes place in the grounds of Dover College. The last event is a banquet held at the Maison Dieu or Town Hall.

Dover Castle

There have been defence works here since the iron age. The Saxon fortifications, built by Harold in 1064, gave way to a Norman castle, which shared the hilltop with a Roman Pharos or lighthouse and a Saxon church, St Mary in Castro.

Henry II put up the first stone walls and, in 1180, the keep, the largest in Britain after the Tower of London and Colchester Castle. The castle was garrisoned in 1185 and remained so until 1958. Some walls are up to 21 feet thick (6.4 metres), with rooms within, and there are over twenty-five rooms in the keep, including a chapel. There is an exhibition of weaponry in one of the halls and a model of the battle of Waterloo takes up much of the space in another. Note, too, Edward III's Cotton Gate (between the keep and the church), the Constable Tower, huge and thirteenth-century, St John's Tower of the same period and Purcell's Tower. There are subterranean passages begun in the thirteenth century and extended during the Napoleonic Wars and in 1940. By the Canon Gate is a large cannon known as Queen Elizabeth's Pocket Pistol, given by Emperor Charles V to Henry VIII in 1544.

The castle is open at the following times: March and October, weekdays 9.30 to 5.30, Sundays 2 to 5.30; April, daily 9.30 to 5.30; May to September, daily 9.30 to 7; November to February, weekdays 9.30 to 4, Sundays 2 to 4.

The cruciform church of **St Mary in Castro** is one of the country's most complete examples of Saxon work, built in the eleventh century of Roman materials. Roofless from the eighteenth century, it served as a coal store, but Sir Gilbert Scott restored it in the 1860s (though he was not responsible for the incongruous mosaics) and it has been the garrison church ever since then.

The remarkable **Pharos** by the garrison church dates from the first or second century AD and may well be the oldest building in Britain; the top storey is fifteenth-century. Originally far higher, the Pharos was matched by a similar one on the Western Heights. They shone across the Channel, where there was a third Pharos near Boulogne.

Port Burgoyne lies just to the north of the castle, built in 1861 to improve the defences and designed to hide men and equipment in a similar fashion to the Western Heights; the idea was to be able to surprise an enemy with the numbers of troops available.

The town

On the corner of the High Street and Ladywell is situated the **Maison Dieu Hall,** part of the town hall buildings, and originally known as the hospital of St Mary. Founded by Hubert de Burgh, Constable of Dover Castle, in 1203, it was a hostel for pilgrims and, later, soldiers. By 1227 it had a chapel, now a courtroom. Another hall, built on to the south side during Edward I's reign and measuring 120 feet by 30 feet (36.6 metres by 9.1 metres), is the main hall that survives today. Used for various purposes after the Dissolution, it was bought by Dover Corporation in 1834 and subsequently restored rather badly. The arms and armour date from the sixteenth century and are on loan from the Tower of London. There are good stained glass windows depicting the history of Dover in the Connaught Hall. The colours are those of the Cinque Ports Volunteers, raised in the late eighteenth century and disbanded in 1814.

The **museum** entrance is situated in Ladywell. Open every day except Wednesdays, it has a large and fascinating collection of items of local and natural history dating from Roman times to the present day. Admission is free.

The library is next door to Maison Dieu, on the left. Known as **Maison Dieu House,** it was built in 1665 for the Admiralty Victualling Agent. The main information centre is between Maison Dieu Hall and the library. Cross the road from the library and walk up Effingham Crescent to **Dover College,** the co-educational public school. The college incorporates remains of the Priory of St Martin, which stood on the same site: the large Norman refectory is still used; the old twelfth-century guest house, once known as King's Chamber, is the college chapel; and the twelfth-century priory gatehouse is also preserved. The college grounds are private but parties or groups are admitted on application to the Bursar.

Coming down Norman Road back to Priory Road, the tiny **Chapel of St Edmund** is across the road on the right. Consecrated in 1253, and only 28 feet (8.5 metres) long and 14 feet (4.3 metres) wide, it is said to be the only surviving example in Britain of a chapel consecrated by an English saint (St Richard of Chichester) to another English saint (St Edmund of Abingdon). They were the first two scholars of Oxford to be canonised. The chapel, lost for centuries, was rediscovered after a bombing raid destroyed adjacent buildings in 1943. Restoration was completed in 1968. The glass-covered cavity in the floor to the right of the altar is, almost certainly, where St Richard's bowels were interred, as they were deemed precious relics. No one knows where the rest of his body is.

From St Edmund's chapel turn left down Priory Road, past the roundabout into York Street. Turn left into New Street to the special building housing Dover's latest treasure, the **Roman Painted House.**

The Painted House was discovered by the Kent Archaeological Rescue Unit in 1970 and was opened to the public in May 1977. It was probably a town house of *c.* AD 200 and may have belonged to a senior official, possibly connected with the Roman fleet. It is said to have a more complete area of Roman wall painting still in its original position than anywhere else north of the Alps. Part of the house was demolished when the Romans built the defensive wall which can be clearly seen. It is open daily, March to November, 10 to 6 (closed December to February). An admission fee is charged.

Continue to the other end of New Street and turn right into Cannon Street to the **parish church of St Mary the Virgin.** There was a Saxon church on this site and St Mary's is mentioned in the Domesday Book. The tower is Norman, though the spire is eighteenth-century, and the church was rebuilt in 1843. A sundial on the south wall of the tower is dated 1656. Inside the church some of the original Norman work can be seen. On the galleries are the arms of William and Mary and of Trinity House. The three-manual organ by Brown of Canterbury was installed in 1878.

Back in Cannon Street, past New Street and into Biggin Street, the visitor is soon back at Maison Dieu.

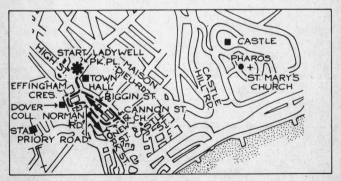

Dover

51

7. The Sandwich group

WALMER

Walmer probably means 'the (Roman) fortification by the sea', from the Saxon, and some Roman remains have been found. Though never important, Walmer became a non-corporate Limb of Sandwich about 1350. It became part of the borough of Deal in 1935.

St Mary Old Church, the original parish church in Church Street, is Norman and has interesting zigzag decoration, typical of the period. Close by in the churchyard is **Walmer Court.** Only the flinted ruins remain of this semi-fortified, originally moated, eleventh-century manor-house of the d'Auberville family.

Walmer Castle was one of three built by Henry VIII about 1540 after the break with Rome to protect the Channel coastline from invasion, the others being at Deal and Sandown. Typically Tudor in design, the castle comprised a circular keep surrounded by a sunken passage, and massive outer walls with four huge bastions. Since the early nineteenth century it has been the official residence of the Lord Warden of the Cinque Ports. Its character has been changed by its various residents, notably William Pitt, or rather by his niece, Lady Hester Stanhope, who acted as his housekeeper and landscaped the gardens. The Duke of Wellington, another Lord Warden, entertained Queen Victoria and Prince Albert here and died in 1852 within the castle. Sir Robert Menzies, the late Lord Warden, lived here when he was in England. The small museum is well worth visiting. The castle is open all year except Mondays (but open bank holiday Mondays), March and October weekdays 9.30 to 5.30, Sundays 2 to 5.30; April daily 9.30 to 5.30; May to September daily 9.30 to 7; November to February weekdays 9.30 to 4, Sundays 2 to 4. There is an admission charge.

DEAL
Population 26,120.

Deal is probably where Julius Caesar landed in 54 BC, but not much is known about the place before its inclusion as a non-corporate Limb of Sandwich in 1229. It was a favourite landing place: Thomas Becket returned from exile through Deal, Richard I returned from the Crusades, the pretender Perkin Warbeck landed forces here in 1495 and Anne of Cleves arrived in 1540.

Deal has prospered with time. Sandwich declined when the river Stour silted up, so Deal took its place, becoming a supply depot fortified by Henry VIII, and then a naval base. William III granted a charter to the town in 1699.

St Leonard's church (Upper Deal), a basically Norman church, was in the centre of old Deal. The west tower with its distinctive cupola was built in 1684 and the church was enlarged in 1819. The fine west end, the Pilots' Gallery, is a reminder of the town's associations with the sea.

The **Maritime and Local History Museum** is at 22 St George's Road in Deal proper, around the corner from the nineteenth-century Town Hall in the High Street. It is usually open daily from 2 to 5. There is an admission charge.

The **Time Ball Tower** on the seafront was built in 1854. It had on its roof a vertical 14-foot (4.2-metre) shaft with a large ball on the top. A weathervane capped the whole structure. Greenwich Observatory was connected by direct electric current. Every day the ball was raised at 12.58 p.m. and dropped at precisely 1 p.m., thus giving the correct Greenwich Mean Time to all shipping in the Dover straits. The service ceased in 1927 with the improvement in radio communications. The Time Ball Tower is now an information centre.

Middle Street and High Street possess a number of eighteenth-century houses, many showing the influence of Dutch building styles brought by Protestant refugees from Holland. There are more examples in Sandwich. The remarkable Elizabeth Carter, classical scholar and friend of Dr Samuel Johnson, lived in what is now the Charter House Hotel from 1762 to 1806.

Deal Castle was one of three castles built by Henry VIII about 1540 to protect the Channel coastline from invasion (the other two are Walmer and the ruined Sandown, just to the north of Deal). Here a circular keep with six bastions was surrounded by a deep passage, and then by a curtain wall with six more, offset bastions, to give all-round cover, but squat, to make them difficult targets for ships. Deal was the largest of the three and its interior is almost as it was originally. It has 145 gun ports. It was never used for its original purpose, although in the Civil War it changed hands twice. It is open in March and October, weekdays 9.30 to 5.30, Sundays 2 to 5.30; April daily 9.30 to 5.30; May to September daily 9.30 to 7; November to February, weekdays 9.30 to 4, Sundays 2 to 4. There is an admission charge.

SANDWICH
Population 4500. Early closing Wednesday. Market day, Thursday.

Sandwich may have been at one time the most important of the Cinque Ports: the Domesday Survey showed that the hundred of Sandwich was owned by Christchurch College, Canterbury, that there was the massive total of 383 houses and that Sandwich, like Dover, supplied twenty ships for the king's service each year. It was probably the seventh largest town in England, and in Kent second only to Canterbury.

Well situated on the Stour, Sandwich developed as a port in Saxon times while Richborough (the Roman fortress and port of *Rutupiae*) declined as the sea receded. Edward the Confessor and Edward IV used the town as a base. At the siege of Calais (1346-7) Sandwich provided twenty-two ships and 504 men.

The town received a charter from Henry II in 1155. Heylas de Kingeston was the first recorded mayor in 1226. Non-corporate Limbs were Deal, Walmer, Stonar, Sarre and Brightlingsea (Essex) and there was one corporate Limb, Fordwich, Canterbury's port, further up the Stour. From 1100 to 1420 or so Sandwich was one of the principal ports of the country, particularly for wine and wool. There were French raids from time to time. Sandwich was sacked in 1216 and twice more before the last attack in 1457, when the mayor, John Drury, was murdered when four thousand Frenchmen raided the town. To commemorate the deed, the Mayor of Sandwich wears a full black robe and his chain of office is ornamented with black bows.

Sandwich declined as a port from the sixteenth century onwards because of silting up. Elizabeth I encouraged the settlement of Flemish and Huguenot refugees, who revitalised Sandwich as they introduced market gardening and weaving into the community. In more recent days the town has become particularly well known for its golf courses, notably Royal St George.

Park at the quay. Today, the river is shallow, the quay nearly neglected. Providing a backdrop to the quay is the **Fisher Gate,** the only remaining town gate, fourteenth-century in construction, though the top half was rebuilt in 1571. A stone under the archway details its history. Walk through Fisher Gate to Upper Strand Street. On the corner is the Old Custom House, whose outer brickwork is eighteenth-century, although the building is far older. Before turning left, glance down Fisher Street, full of quaint cottages, and with the George and Dragon Inn on the right. Down Upper Strand Street at the end is The Salutation, a twentieth-century house in Queen Anne style designed by Sir Edwin Lutyens. Turn right here, into Hogs Corner. Across the churchyard stands the **parish church of St Clement.**

The oldest part of the church is the arcaded Norman tower, which dates from *c.* 1100. Enter the church by the two-storeyed north porch. St Clement's is cruciform in layout, the chancel being in the Early English style, the nave fifteenth-century.

Notice the early fifteenth-century font, which bears the arms of the Cinque Ports and those of a local family, possibly that of Archdeacon Hallum who probably gave the font to the church. In the north choir aisle is St Margaret's Chapel with a medieval tiled floor. Note the hagioscope between the chapel and the high altar, which has an original stone altar slab. There is a still functioning misericord in the choirstalls. Note, too, the unusual Norman tympanum above the doorway to the spiral tower staircase.

The west end of the church is dominated by the twin organ cases. The organ was given by Sir Aynsley Bridgland in 1951. The console is on the north side of the choir.

To the west of the north entrance there are stairs which go up to the ancient priest's room above the porch.

Rejoin Knightrider Street, which, within 200 yards (180 metres), takes the visitor to **Mill Wall,** part of the town's ramparts named after a vanished windmill. The ramparts still encircle a large part

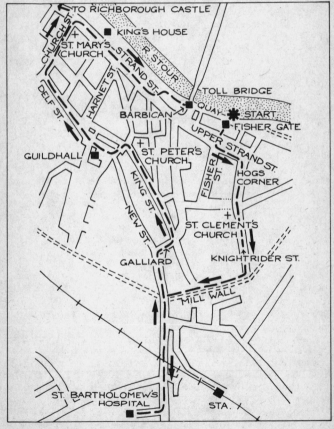

Sandwich

of the town, their steep sides leading down to what was once the moat. Turn right, keeping the bowls club to the right, walk down busy New Street and turn left. Over the railway tracks, and about 300 yards (275 metres) further along the right-hand side, is the ancient **Hospital of St Bartholomew**, a large courtyard surrounded by delightful almshouses, with St Bartholomew's chapel in the middle. Founded probably in thanksgiving for a victory over the French on St Bartholomew's Day, the original travellers' hostel was reconstituted for use as a hospital for the 'old and decayed' of Sandwich. Sixteen single Brothers or Sisters have their names and years of joining put above the doors to their almshouses. Each St Bartholomew's Day children run round the chapel for a Bartholomew's bun or biscuit. The Master for the forthcoming year is chosen by the Chairman of Trustees by 'pricking' the list of Brothers with a bodkin. The Early English style chapel, restored by Sir Gilbert Scott, has a table tomb with a thirteenth-century effigy said to be Sir Henry Sandwich, a Lord Warden of the Cinque Ports in Henry III's day.

Rejoin New Street where Mill Wall meets it. On the right by Mill Wall is the Delf Stream. It was built to supply Sandwich with pure water and is known to have existed in 1206. It can be seen again in Delf Street where it is diverted between some buildings by Horse Pond Sluice. Continuing up New Street, turn right into the Galliard, then immediately left into King Street. The old Dutch House here is the best example of Protestant Dutch design. Follow the street round to the left to **St Peter's church,** now redundant, which stands on the probable site of a Saxon church. St Peter's was destroyed by invaders in the thirteenth century and rebuilt by monks. The aisles were widened in the fourteenth century. In 1661 the central tower collapsed. The church was taken over by the Dutch refugees. Now it is unsafe and is no longer used for services, although the curfew bell is still rung.

Return to New Street, to the Guildhall. At this end of New Street, at Number 20, is the house of Tom Paine, author of *The Rights of Man,* who lived there in 1759. Look, too, at Whitefriars, all that remains of a medieval community which lived there probably until the Dissolution of the monasteries. The White Friars' seals are kept in the Guildhall.

A twentieth-century exterior masks the lovely 1579 interior of the **Guildhall.** The new wing, which includes the stately archway, was added recently. On the ground floor is the Court Hall, with fine, carved panelling and a fourteenth-century screen. There are portraits and pictures, notably of Charles II. The halberds hanging from the ceiling belonged to the Cinque Ports fleet and were, at one time, carried before the judge when quarter sessions were held here. Above are the Council Chamber, with its superb seventeenth-century mayor's chair, and a mayor's parlour. There is also a small museum, where it is possible to see the charter granted by King Charles II and a quarter of the canopy held by the Barons of the Cinque Ports at George III's coronation in 1761.

From the Guildhall, walk down Delf Street, noting the reappearance and disappearance via Horse Pond Sluice of Delf Stream. Turn into quaint Church Street until on the corner with Strand Street **St Mary's church** is reached.

St Mary's was the earliest site of Christian worship in Sandwich, possibly seventh-century. Although rebuilt by Emma, wife of Canute, after destruction by the Danes the earliest part of this building is Norman, glimpsed at the west end. Much is early thirteenth-century with nineteenth-century additions, including windows. Its bare and slightly depressing interior reflects a stormy history, for it was attacked and damaged by the French in 1257 and 1457. It suffered from an earthquake in 1578 and this may have caused the collapse of the central tower in 1667. The Friends of St Mary's saved the church from demolition earlier this century. The very rusty old chest which stands near the entrance is a medieval Peter's Pence box, which collected money for the papal tribute before Henry VIII stopped it. There are very few such boxes still in existence.

Leaving St Mary's, turn right into Strand Street. On the left is the entrance to **King's House** (or Lodging). The unpleasant gates once belonged to the town gaol. The house is early sixteenth-century, though the front windows are eighteenth-century. It is said that Henry VIII paid a visit in 1534 and that in 1573 Queen Elizabeth I viewed the fleet from a bow window here.

Down Harnet Street, to the right, at Number 38, is the **Precinct Toy Collection,** with toys from the nineteenth century to the present day. It is open Easter to September from 10 to 5 on weekdays, on Sundays from 2 to 5. There is an admission charge.

Returning to Strand Street, find one of the little passages leading down to the old quay and wander along to the Barbican and Tollbridge beside the river. The **Bridgegate** or **Barbican** is Tudor. The present bridge, the third, was built at the turn of this century. It is only a short way from here back to the car park.

Richborough Castle is a mile from Sandwich, off Richborough Road. The first-century Roman fortification, originally known as *Rutupiae,* stands on a low hill above the river. The principal port of Britain, it formed part of a chain of forts along the south-east coast under the control of the Count of the Saxon Shore in the fourth century. When the Wantsum Channel between the Isle of Thanet and the mainland silted up, Richborough ceased to be useful. Much excavation has been done; there is a museum on the site. It is open every day 9.30 to 5.30 between May and August, though only on Sunday afternoons between September and April. There is an admission charge.

Pegwell Bay is to the north of Sandwich, almost an extension of Ramsgate. Here is the supposed point — now half a mile (800 metres) inland and marked with a cross — where St Augustine landed in AD 597. Today, it is better known as a hoverport.

8. Other Cinque Port towns of interest

FORDWICH

Just to the south of the village of Sturry on the A28 a mile or so east of Canterbury is Fordwich, the old port on the Stour for Canterbury. The Abbot of St Augustine's, Canterbury, was lord of the manor and the stone for Canterbury Cathedral was sent to this port from Caen in France. At the time of the Domesday survey Fordwich, possibly Jutish in origin, had been established for several centuries and was one of only eight burghs in the whole of Kent. It held several pre-Conquest charters and became an incorporated borough under a charter granted by Henry II. It had, uniquely among the Cinque Ports, a Merchant Guild. The Municipal Corporation Act of 1884 abolished its borough status.

Fordwich was probably bound to its Head Port, Sandwich, as early as the Norman conquest. This led to friction between the Cinque Ports and St Augustine's Abbey, as the Ports had exemption from dues but the Abbey held the lordship of the manor and wanted proper payment for the use of its port. Christchurch Priory, Canterbury, also wanted landing rights in Fordwich. The dissolution of the monasteries finished the argument. From Tudor times the river declined until by the eighteenth century Fordwich had ceased to be a port.

Today, Fordwich is a small but captivating village almost unspoilt by twentieth-century buildings. It still pays ship money of 17p a year to Sandwich. It also has a Mayor Deputy to represent the Limb at gatherings of the Cinque Ports.

The **parish church of St Mary** stands on the site of an early eleventh-century church. It was built not long after the Conquest but was altered in the thirteenth and fourteenth centuries. It contains eighteenth-century box pews and the Fordwich Stone, a block of oolitic stone 5½ feet (1.7 metres) long in the north aisle, said to date from Norman times. There is also a ship's model of a 'carrick' of about 1470, built in memory of those killed in the First World War.

The **Court Hall** or Moot Hall was probably built c. 1544, a timber-framed building with a kingpost roof. It houses a small but irregularly opened museum. The top storey was the courtroom, and the small gaol, just big enough for three prisoners, occupied part of the ground floor. Among the relics on show is a ducking stool, which was often used for scolding wives. Next door can be seen the old crane house, which had its part to play on such occasions as well as in the loading and unloading of barges.

FAVERSHAM
Population 14,990. Early closing Thursday. Market days Friday and Saturday.

Faversham lies nine miles north-west of Canterbury, up a creek which flows into the Swale. It existed in Saxon times and in a charter of AD 811 was referred to as a 'royal ville'. It was an incorporated Limb of Dover by 1229. King Stephen founded an abbey here, and he was buried there with his queen, Matilda, and their son, Prince Eustace. The abbey was destroyed at the dissolution of the monasteries *c.* 1540. Nearby Davington Priory housed an order of Benedictine nuns. In 1688 James II was captured by local fishermen when his boat was driven ashore here.

Faversham enjoyed considerable privileges and was a noted trading port; its oyster fishing industry existed for seven hundred years until the 1930s. Gunpowder was manufactured here from 1570 to 1935 and brewing has been carried on in the town for over two hundred years. Flemish and Huguenot refugees settled here in the sixteenth and seventeenth centuries. It has never been in the front line of battle like the other Cinque Ports.

Although it now comes under Swale District Council, Faversham retains its town council and mayoralty.

The **parish church of St Mary of Charity** has Norman arcades at the west end of the nave. It was rebuilt in the eighteenth century and restored in the nineteenth. This massive church has double-aisled transepts; there are barely half a dozen examples of this in England. The tower and steeple date from 1791, built by Charles Beazley after the Wren style of an east London church. Note the misericords in the choirstalls, the wall paintings on the south-east pillar of the north transept, a 1754 organ case and a number of interesting brasses.

Queen Elizabeth's Old Grammar School, north-west of the parish church, a timber-framed building of 1587, which still has some of the original benches, was a school until 1880 and has been a Masonic hall since 1887. The **Guildhall** dominates the market place. It was built *c.* 1570 as a market hall but was converted into the Guildhall in 1604. In 1819 the upper part was rebuilt. Most of the buildings facing the Guildhall around the market place are at least two hundred years old.

Chart Gunpowder Mills date from *c.* 1760 and are claimed to be the oldest of their kind in the world. The big waterwheel and several other items of machinery can be seen.

West Street leads off from the market place and has many delightful sixteenth- and seventeenth-century houses. The Ship

Inn is Tudor behind its more modern frontage. Abbey Street, at the end of Court Street, has had much of its original sixteenth-century character restored in recent years.

Ospringe adjoins Faversham and where Ospringe Street (A2) meets London Road stands the fifteenth-century **Maison Dieu** on the site of an early thirteenth-century hospital which provided shelter for travellers and a refuge for the sick or old. Standing on the London-Dover road, it was used by royalty, notably Henry III, Edward I and Edward II. Upstairs is an archaeological museum, downstairs a historical museum. It is open daily, 9.30 to 4 November to February, 9.30 to 5.30 the rest of the year (closed 1 to 2). There is an admission charge.

MARGATE
Population 49,730. Early closing Thursday. Market days Thursday and Friday.

Margate now includes four non-corporate Limbs of Dover — Woodchurch, St John's, Birchington and Margate — which finally became one incorporated member in 1857, the first for 150 years. A small village until the late fifteenth century, Margate became the point of embarkation for Holland. Those wounded at Waterloo in 1815 were brought back to Margate. It probably owes its popularity as a seaside resort not only to its sandy beaches but also because Benjamin Beale first introduced bathing machines there about 1750.

RAMSGATE
Population 40,070. Early closing Thursday. Market day Friday.

The 'gate' probably refers to the gap in the chalk cliffs where the town is sited. It was a small fishing village, a non-corporate Limb of Sandwich. It is not mentioned in the Cinque Ports records until the fourteenth century. It did not expand much until the eighteenth century. Troops embarked for the Waterloo campaign there; so did George IV on his way to Hanover in 1821. Ramsgate finally achieved incorporated status in 1884.

General bibliography

There are numerous books on individual Cinque Ports but for an introduction to the subject, the following are useful :

Brentnall, Margaret. *The Cinque Ports and Romney Marsh.* John Gilford, 1972.

Hammond, R. J. W. (ed). *East Sussex Coast.* Ward, Lock & Co., 1967

Jessup, R. and F. *The Cinque Ports.* B. T. Batsford, 1952.

Mais, S. P. B. *The Land of the Cinque Ports.* Christopher Johnson, 1949.

Millward, R., and Robinson, A. *South-east England : The Channel Coastline.* Macmillan, 1973.

Murray, Walter J. C. *Romney Marsh.* Robert Hale, 1972

Newman, John. *North-east and East Kent.* Penguin, 1969.

Williams, Geoffrey. *The Heraldry of the Cinque Ports.* David & Charles, 1971.

Index

Titles available in the Discovering series

Antique Maps
Archaeology in Denmark
Archaeology in England and Wales
Avon
Backgammon
Banknotes
Battlefields of Scotland
Beekeeping
Bird Courtship
Bird Song
Bird Watching
Brasses and Brassrubbing
British Cavalry Regiments
British Ponies
Burns Country
Cambridgeshire
Carts and Wagons
Castle Combe
Castles in England and Wales
Cathedrals
Chapels and Meeting Houses
Chess
Christmas Customs and Folklore
Churches
The Cinque Ports
Cleveland
Country Crafts
Country Walks in North London
Craft of the Inland Waterways
Derbyshire and the Peak District
Ecology
Edged Weapons
Embroidery of the Nineteenth Century
English Dialects
English Furniture
English Literary Associations
Essex
Famous Battles: Peninsular War
Farmhouse Cheese
Farm Museums and Farm Parks
Folklore and Customs of Love and Marriage
Folklore of Plants
French and German Military Uniforms
Gardening for the Handicapped
Geology
Hallmarks on English Silver
Hampshire and the New Forest
Herbs
Horse Brasses
Horse-drawn Carriages
Horse-drawn Commercial Vehicles
Horse-drawn Transport of the British Army
Industrial Archaeology and History
Kent
Kings and Queens
Lancashire

Leicestershire and Rutland
Lincolnshire
Local History
London's Canals
London's Guilds and Liveries
London for Children
London Street Names
Lost Canals
Lost Railways
Mah-jong
Maritime Museums and Historic Ships
Mechanical Music
Military Traditions
Model Soldiers
Mottoes
Northamptonshire
Northumbria
Nottinghamshire
Old Aeroplanes
Old Bicycles
Old Motor Cycles
Pantomime
Picture Postcards
Place Names
Quantocks
Regional Archaeology series:
   North-Eastern England
   South-Eastern England
   South-Western England
   The Ridgeway
Rules for Wargaming
Salop
South Yorkshire
Space and Astronomy
Staffordshire
Stately Homes
Statues in Cent. & N. England
Statues in S. England
Suffolk
Surnames
Sussex
Thames and Chilterns
Theatre Ephemera
Topiary
Towns
Toys and Toy Museums
Trams and Tramways
Walks in Buckinghamshire
Walks in the New Forest
Walks in Wessex Towns
Walks in West Kent
Walks in West Sussex
Watermills
Westward Stage
Windmills
Your Family Tree
Your Old House

From your bookseller or from Shire Publications Ltd, Cromwell House, Church Street, Princes Risborough, Aylesbury, Bucks, HP17 9AJ, U.K.